WORLD'S WACKIEST RIDDLE BOOK

EVELYN JONES

Illustrations by
DENNIS KENDRICK

STERLING PUBLISHING CO., INC.
New York

To Jeannie Colligan and crazy conversation

Many thanks to the patient friends on whom I tried out hundreds of riddles while writing this book: Amy, Phyl, Bucky, Sherry, Meredith, Donna Lee and her pupils at Stratham, N.H. Memorial School, Zach, Tom, Judy and Ann Rehner, Eric, Matthew and Christopher Brown.

Library of Congress Cataloging-in-Publication Data Available

10   9   8   7   6   5   4   3   2   1

Published in 2004 by Sterling Publishing Co., Inc.
387 Park Avenue South
New York, NY 10016
Based on the previously published *World's Wackiest Riddle Book* by Evelyn Jones
© 1986 by Sterling Publishing Co., Inc.
Distributed in Canada by Sterling Publishing
c/o Canadian Manda Group
One Atlantic Avenue, Suite 105
Toronto, Ontario, M6K 3E7, Canada
Distributed in Great Britain and Europe by Chris Lloyd at
Orca Book Services
Stanley House, Fleets Lane, Poole BH15 3AJ, England
Distributed in Australia by Capricorn Link (Australia) Pty Ltd.
P.O. Box 704, Windsor, NSW 27566, Australia

Sterling ISBN 1-4027-0924-2

CONTENTS

FAST & FREAKY

1

Why do witches wear green eye shadow?
It matches their teeth.

Why do witches carry cats on their broomsticks?
Because elephants get airsick.

What do little ghosts wear?
Pillowcases.

What color are they?
Boo!

What do little ghosts wear on their feet?
Boo-ties.

What game do they play?
Peek-a-boo!

What ghost lost her sheep?
Little Boo-Peep.

What did the ghoul use to wash his hair?
Sham-boo.

What do you get if you cross a pony and a ghost?
Whinny the Boo.

Where do little ghosts go swimming?
In Lake Eerie.

What kind of bats swing upside down?
Acro-bats.

What kind of bats know their ABC's?
Alpha-bats.

Why are demons always skinny?
They get lots of exorcise.

How do skeletons deliver the mail?
By Boney Express.

What did the little vampire win in the Horribles Parade?
The boo-by prize.

What is the vampires' favorite city?
Boo-charest.

Why did the psychic go into the hospital?
To have an apparition.

What did the little vampire say when they handed it the prize?
"Fang you very much!"

Why did Dracula visit an astrologer?
To get his horror-scope.

THE JOINT IS JUMPING

What happened to the frog who ate too much?
  He turned into a hoppopotamus.

What happened to the frog who sat on a telephone?
  He grew up to be a bellhop.

What happened to the frog who broke its leg?
  It was hopless.

What does a frog use to sit on?
  Toadstools.

How do army frogs march?
"*Hop, 2, 3, 4!*"

Why did the frog get kicked out of
the navy?
He kept jumping ship.

Why did the frog sit on the lily pad?
Her sofa was being repaired.

What happens when frogs get
married?
They live hoppily ever after.

What is Dracula's favorite food?
Hungarian ghoul-ash.

What does a witch put in her coffee?
Sugar and scream.

What is a mermaid's favorite sandwich?
Peanut butter and jellyfish.

Why are Italian chefs so smart?
They always use their noodles.

What does a hungry giant order for lunch?
Ham on rhi-noceros!

What's it like to eat breakfast with Scrooge?
It's a gruel-ing experience.

ALL IN A DAY'S WORK

2

Why did the judge send for a safecracker?
The jury was deadlocked.

Why did the judge send for a locksmith?
The key witness was missing.

Why did the secret agent whisper "1, 2, 3, 4,
5, 6, 7 . . ."?
He was a counter-spy.

Why did the secret agent take two aspirins
and go to bed?
He had a code in his head.

When does a lawyer make coffee?
When he has sufficient grounds.

Why was the calendar so sad?
Its days were numbered.

What color is bad luck for sailors?
Maroon.

Why is a tired soldier like a broken-down cathedral?
Both have fallen arches.

Why did the carpenter hire a secretary?
To file his nails.

What happens when two army officers collide?
A Major disaster.

When do pilots fly close to the ground?
In so-low flights.

How does a train conductor sneeze?
"Ahhhh choo-choo!"

What kind of saws and nails are useless to a carpenter?
Seesaws and toenails.

What holds up a solar house?
Sunbeams.

Why did the boxer like his new job?
He got to punch the time clock.

What do you call a couple of salesmen who go to jail?
Sell-mates.

What kind of people should never get wrapped up in their work?
The ones who raise boa constrictors.

PURE CORN

Why does a farmer think the letter R is amazing?
> *It can change a pea into a pear.*

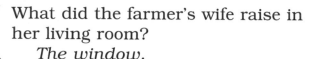

What did the farmer's wife raise in her living room?
> *The window.*

What does a farmer do when he finds a hole in his garden?
> *He sows it.*

What's the difference between a proud farmer and a pirate?
> *The farmer treasures his berries and the pirate buries his treasures.*

How do grapes grow in California?
> *Just vine, thanks.*

How does a farmer mend his overalls?
With cabbage patches.

When a ewe marries a ram, what
does he become?
Her butt-er half.

When does a horse talk?
Whinny wants to.

What has four wheels and honks?
A goose on a skateboard.

When is mealtime in the henhouse?
Eggsactly six o' clock.

Where in town do needleworkers live?
On the outskirts.

Why do dressmakers like the wide-open spaces?
So they don't feel hemmed in.

Is it hard to learn to sew?
No, it's thimble.

How did the teacher get locked out of the music room?
His keys were left on the piano.

What kind of music can you play with a shoehorn?
Footnotes.

How does a musician brush his teeth?
With a tuba toothpaste.

Why are termites successful in the theater?
They bring down the house.

Why did the actor take his baseball bat to
New York?
He wanted to make a hit on Broadway.

When is a basketball player like a baby?
When he dribbles.

Why did the actor envy the artist?
*The artist had no trouble drawing big
crowds.*

When is an absent-minded circus owner like
a nervous actor?
When he forgets his lions.

What did the lumberjack do after he cut
down the tree?
He took a bough.

What happens to spoons when they work
too hard?
They go stir crazy!

What happened when the magician did a
scary trick?

His hare stood on end.

3   WHAT'S THE QUESTION?

In these great new riddles you don't need to find the right answers. You get them to start with. What you need to find are the right questions! They're tough, but lots of fun. Good luck!

A: *Mount Vernon.*
Q: Before riding Vernon the horse, what must you do?

A: *7-Up.*
Q: What happens in Snow White's cottage when the alarm clock rings?

A: *Overlap.*
Q: Where is the belly button located?

A: *Tulips.*
Q: What's located beneath your nose?

A: *Overshoes.*
Q: Where are the ankles located?

A: *Nose drops.*
Q: What happens when the bridge of your nose collapses?

A: *Marionette.*
Q: Has Marion had her breakfast?

A: *William Tell.*
Q: What does bigmouth William do when he hears a secret?

A: *Wilbur and Orville.*
Q: Name two brothers who are never wrong.

A: *A sandwitch.*
Q: Who casts spells in the Sahara Desert?

A: *Dr. Pepper.*
Q: Who married Nurse Salt?

A: *Norwegian, Swede, and Dane.*
Q: Name two Scandinavians and a large dog.

A: *A happy medium.*
Q: What do you get if you tell jokes to a psychic?

A: *A hardened criminal.*
Q: What do you call a thief who fell into cement?

A: *In a class by himself.*
Q: How do you describe a boy who's kept after school?

A: *Alligator.*
Q: Guess what happened when Alec the cat met a canary?

A: *Ran out of time.*
Q: What did the Hickory Dickory mouse do at 1 o'clock?

A: *A Siberian husky.*

Q: Who won the Russian weight-lifting contest?

A: *Calm, cool, and collected.*

Q: How does your stamp album feel when it's kept in the refrigerator?

A: *"That's uncanny!"*

Q: What did Old Mother Hubbard say when she found her cupboard empty?

A: *Tom Sawyer.*

Q: How did Tom know she swiped the cookies?

A: *Nitty-gritty.*

Q: What kind of wool do you get from muddy sheep?

A: *Tycoon.*

Q: What do you call a raccoon that wears bow ties?

4

PET TALK

Which dogs bark more, old ones or young ones?
It's about arf and arf.

Why does a mouse like the letter S?
It makes the cat scat!

What goes "Zzzzz, meow, zzzzz, meow"?
Someone taking a cat nap.

When does a cat like a cat nap?
After a nip at the catnip.

How can a dog get rid of ticks?
By taking off its wristwatch.

TUFFY THE CAT

A: *Defense.*
Q: What does Tuffy the Cat sit on all night?

A: *Defeat, detail, and defer.*
Q: What makes Tuffy so handsome?

A: *Dismay.*
Q: When will Tuffy get out of school?

A: *Descent.*
Q: What's the difference between a cat and a skunk?

What should you feed an overweight cat?
Slender Vittles.

What do you get if you cross bubble gum, a hen, and a dog?
Snap, cackle, and pup.

What animals do scouts take on overnight trips?
Pup tents and first-aid kits.

What part of a tent is hardest to keep clean?
The ground floor.

How did pioneer puppies go west?
In waggin' trains.

THE JOINT IS JUMPING

What has big eyes, green skin, and lives alone?
Hermit the frog.

How does a frog cross a busy street?
He hops a bus.

Why don't frogs make good workers?
They're too hoppy-go-lucky.

What should you say when you meet a toad?
"Wart's new?"

Why do dogs run in circles?
It's hard to run in squares.

Why didn't the church mouse live in the steeple?
She didn't a-spire that high.

What do you get if you cross a turtle and a boomerang?
Snappy comebacks.

What do you get if you cross a hen and a parrot?
A bird that uses really fowl language.

SUPERSTARS & OTHER GREATS

5

Why did all the king's men laugh at Humpty Dumpty?
They thought he was a big yolk.

What do you call a sheep that hangs out with 40 thieves?
Ali Baa Baa.

What do you call an elephant that hangs out with 40 thieves?
Ali Babar.

Who was unhappy at the way his suit came back from the cleaners?
Ripped van Wrinkled.

Where can you find a great boxer?
At Muhammad's Alley.

What turkey starred in *Gone With The Wind*?
Clark Gobble.

What's made of chicken and rice and is faster than a speeding bullet?
Chicken Soup-erman.

What was Chicken Souperman's other name?
Cluck Kent.

Who writes mystery stories and blooms in spring?
Edgar Allan Poe-sy.

Will Mrs. Alcott ever write a book called *Little Women?*
No, but Louisa May.

Why did Queen Elizabeth I refuse to marry?
No suitor could suit'er.

What Scottish king was round and had a
hole in the middle?
King Duncan Doughnut.

What flies, does magic, and has no name?
An Unidentified Flying Sorcerer.

What would you call an expert in mud
wrestling?
The Wizard of Ooze.

How do we know Jack and Jill were royalty?
*Because when Jack fell down he broke
his crown.*

Who has six legs, wears a coonskin cap,
and chirps?
Davy Cricket.

MOO-VING RIGHT ALONG

Why did Elsie the Cow go to Hollywood?
To be a moo-vie star.

Did Elsie the Cow get to be a movie star?
No, but she made lots of moo-lah.

What kind of car did Elsie the Cow drive?
A moo-ving van.

What happened when Miss Piggy appeared in a play?
She hogged the stage.

How does the Lone Ranger keep his horse so shiny?
Silver polish.

Why can't Smokey go to the movies?
No one with bear feet is allowed.

What happens to Whistler's Mother when she works too hard?
She goes off her rocker.

What happens to King Kong when he works too hard?

He goes bananas.

Why did the famous spy, Mata Hari, always look so sad?

She was no laughing Mata.

Who invents telephones and carries your luggage?
Alexander Graham Bellhop.

What has a curly tail and a snout, and wears a red, white, and blue costume?
Oinkle Sam.

Who has curly hair and says "Arf, Arf"?
Little Arfin' Annie.

What dog gets rusty if you leave him out in the rain?
Rin Tin Tin.

What's the difference between St. George and Rudolf the Red-Nosed Reindeer?

One slays the dragon and the other's draggin' the sleigh.

Where does Santa stay overnight when he travels?

At ho-ho-hotels.

Why doesn't Santa live at the South Pole?

His reindeer don't like to eat upside down.

6

MR. PRESIDENT, MR. PRESIDENT!

Which president had big sharp teeth?
Jaws Washington.

Which president was a great help to Santa?
Chimney Carter.

Which president made a nice pie for
Washington's birthday?
Cherry Ford.

Which president was orange-flavored?
Sherbet Hoover.

Which president liked to dance?
James Polka.

Which president acted like a clown?
Jester A. Arthur.

Which president was a dentist in his spare time?
Millard Fillmore.

Which president never had to wear a wig?
Hairy Truman.

Which president liked horror films?
Calvin Ghoulidge.

Which president had trouble with the dog-catcher?

Rover Cleveland.

Which president talked like a pig?

Ulysses S. Grunt.

Which president kept Washington, D.C. in stitches?

Zachary Tailor.

LOVE & HISSES

7

What happens when you fall in love with a telephone operator?
She gives you a phone-y line.

What happens when you fall in love with a trashman?
He dumps you.

What happens when you fall in love with a clockmaker?
She two-times you.

What happens when you fall in love with a pastry cook?
He desserts you.

What happens when you fall in love with an artist?
You get the brush.

What happens when you fall in love with a
shoe salesman?
*He walks all over
you.*

UH-OH!

What happens
when you fall in love
with an elevator?
He lets you down.

What happens when
you fall in love with a trench
digger?
You get ditched.

What happens when you fall in love with a
jogger?
You get the run-around.

What happens when you fall in love with an
underwear salesman?
You get the slip.

What happens when you fall in love with a
chauffeur?
You get taken for a ride.

What happens when you fall in love with a
chef?
You get buttered up.

A: *Doe-si-doe.*
Q: What happens when two deer meet at a square dance?

A: *Hoe down.*
Q: What's a farmer's favorite dance?

A: *Despair.*
Q: What comes in handy when you have a flat tire?

A: *Tom Thumb.*

Q: What does Tom do when his car breaks down?

A: *Eavesdropping.*

Q: What's a sign that your roof needs repair?

A: *Bassinet.*

Q: What makes a fisherman happy?

A: *Wishy-washy.*

Q: What do you call laundry day at your fairy godmother's house?

A: *Flying saucers.*
Q: What do flying cups land on?

A: *Mississippi.*
Q: Who's married to Mr. Sippi?

A: *Yard work.*
Q: If you had three feet, what kind of work would you do?

A: *Undersecretary of State.*
Q: Where is the Secretary of State's chair?

A: *A pair of drawers.*
Q: Who were Picasso and Michelangelo?

A: *Chairman of the Bored.*
Q: Who yawns the most?

A: *Afterward.*
Q: Where does "ware" appear in the dictionary?

A: *An outstanding pupil.*
Q: If the teacher makes you stand outside, what are you?

A: *Home Sweet Home.*
Q: What did Hansel and Gretel call the gingerbread house?

A: *It was just a harebrained idea.*

Q: Why did the rabbit start hiding Easter eggs?

A: *Calamity.*

Q: What kind of tea is best to avoid?

A: *Chrysanthemum.*

Q: What flower was named after Christopher Columbus and his mother?

A: *Mohair.*
Q: What does a
balding man want?

A: *Goblet.*
Q: What will a dog
do to steak?

A: *Medium rare.*
Q: What is an unusual
fortune-teller called?

A: *A shady deal.*
Q: What do you get when you play cards
under a chestnut tree?

9

ANIMAL FAIR

What does a parrot say on the Fourth of July?
"Polly want a firecracker!"

What would you call a bird that joins the Ice Capades?
A cheep skate.

Where do woodpeckers conduct their business?
In branch offices.

How do you drive a centipede crazy?
Ask him to put his best foot forward.

Why do bees fly?
They're too buzzy to wait for a bus.

What did the walrus say to the polar bear?
"Have an ice day!"

How do you make a pig fly?
Add e-o-n to its name and it turns into a pigeon.

What did the horses do on Election Day?
They voted neigh.

What do you get if you cross a Boy Scout and a giraffe?
A boy everyone looks up to.

Why do kangaroos make good football
players?
   They're never out of bounds.

What do kangaroos read?
   Pocketbooks.

What do you get if you cross an elephant
with a Model T Ford?
   *Either a cranky elephant or a car with a
   very large trunk.*

What is gray, has large ears, and says squeak, squeak?
An elephant wearing new shoes.

When does an elephant use Ivory Soap?
When he washes his tusks.

Where do little bears sit on a train?
In the cub-oose.

Why do lions roar?
They would feel silly saying "oink, oink."

MOO-VING RIGHT ALONG

What do you get if you cross a cow with a belly dancer?
   Milkshakes.

What do you get from a cow that reads *Reader's Digest*?
   Condensed milk.

What do you get from an invisible cow?
   Evaporated milk.

What do you get from a magician's cow?
   Vanishing cream.

What do you get from an Alaskan cow?
Cold cream.

What do you get from a funny cow?
Cream of wit.

What do you get from a cow that tells bad jokes?
Creamed corn.

Why don't cows like to tell jokes?
Because they're often in a bad moo-ed.

Do cows often graze alone?
Herdly ever.

What do you get if you cross a laughing hyena with an elephant?
   Dr. Chuckle and Mr. Hide.

How come animals can't keep secrets?
   Because pigs squeal, yaks yak, and someone always lets the cat out of the bag.

What's the easiest way to fill a pen?
   Round up a bunch of pigs and push them inside.

How do we know gnus are smarter than dogs?

Because you can't teach an old dog gnu tricks.

Why did the little gnu stay home from school?

She had gnu-monia.

Why should you invite a toad and a gnu to your New Year's Eve party?

So you'll have a Hoppy Gnu Year!

How come fish get so much mail?

Someone is always dropping them a line.

TATERS & GATORS

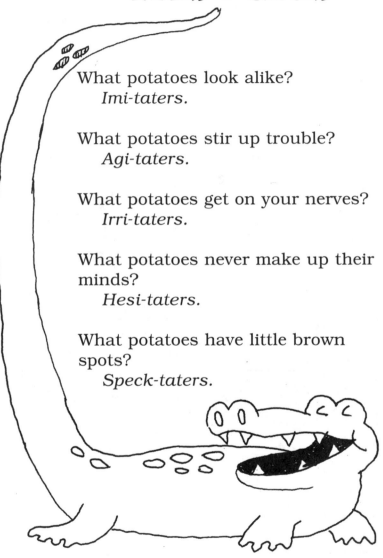

What potatoes look alike?
  Imi-taters.

What potatoes stir up trouble?
  Agi-taters.

What potatoes get on your nerves?
  Irri-taters.

What potatoes never make up their minds?
  Hesi-taters.

What potatoes have little brown spots?
  Speck-taters.

What alligators are very social?
Congre-gators.

What alligators join the navy?
Navi-gators.

What alligators join the FBI?
Investi-gators.

What lizards prefer old-fashioned phones?
Croco-dials.

Why does an octopus need lots of phones?
So it can reach out and touch someone.

What do you get if you cross an octopus
with a clock?
*Either a clock with eight hands or an
octopus that's really ticked off.*

FAMILY TIEƒ

10

I f your mother was very tiny, what would you call her?
Minimum.

If your mother sang like a little bird, what would you call her?
Malarkey.

If your aunt was very old, what would you call her?
Antique.

ANTI-AUNTIE

If your aunt had a big
appetite, what would she be?
An anteater.

If she had an upset stomach,
what would you call her?
Antacid.

If she was always cold, what would
you call her?
Anti-freeze.

If your aunt was very fond of you,
what would she be?
Antidote.

If she thought she was an air-
plane, what would you call her?
Anti-aircraft.

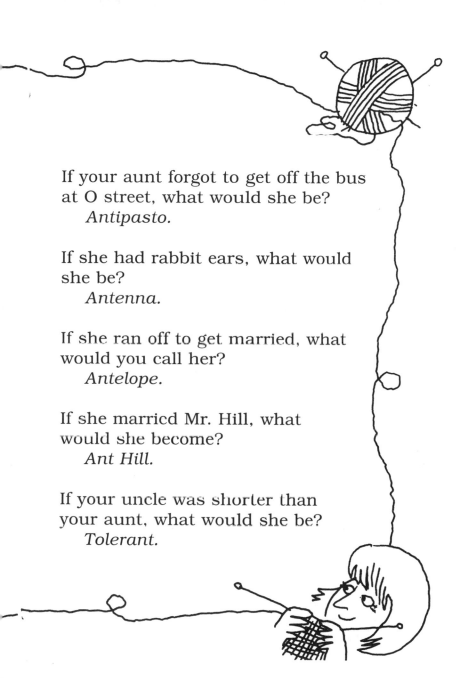

If your aunt forgot to get off the bus at O street, what would she be?
Antipasto.

If she had rabbit ears, what would she be?
Antenna.

If she ran off to get married, what would you call her?
Antelope.

If she married Mr. Hill, what would she become?
Ant Hill.

If your uncle was shorter than your aunt, what would she be?
Tolerant.

If your mother stuck
a feather in her
cap, what would
you call her?
  Macaroni.

If your father was a barber, what would you
call him?
  Parsnips.

If your father loved
pizza with extra
cheese, what would
you call him?
  Parcheesi.

If your father told dumb jokes, what would
you call him?
  Pop Corn.

RHYME TIME

11

What kind of ghost always gives you an argument?
A squabblin' goblin.

What goblin throws the best party?
A ghost host.

What kind of joke makes a violin laugh?
A fiddle riddle.

When Rip Van Winkle woke up after 20 years, what did he have on his face?
A weird beard.

What noise do sleeping lions make?
Roaring snoring!

What do you get when you tell geese too many riddles?
Bonkers honkers!

What does a jellyfish see when it looks in the mirror?
A squishy fishy.

What bear likes ginger ale?
A fizzly grizzly.

What does your dog give you that no one else can?
A pooch smooch.

What do you call a bunch of dopey cows?
A nerd herd.

What do you get if you don't give your taxi driver a tip?
A crabby cabby.

What kind of nose does a fat pig have?
A stout snout.

What did Miss Piggy wear on her head when she went to the party?
A pig wig.

12

SILLY GILLY

What happened when Silly Gilly left her library book outdoors?
In the morning it was over dew.

Why did Silly Gilly pour alphabet soup in her pocket?
She wanted to be a letter carrier.

Why didn't Silly Gilly answer the door?
She thought it was her knees knocking.

What kind of hat did Silly Gilly wear to the auto show?
A hubcap.

What did Silly Gilly get when she bought torn panty hose?
A run for her money.

Why did Silly Gilly put a clock under her desk?
The boss asked her to work overtime.

Why did Silly Gilly tell everyone she was engaged?
Because her boyfriend said he'd give her a ring tonight.

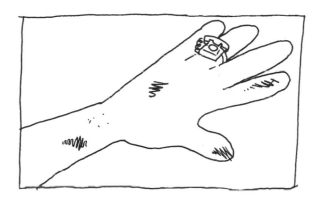

If a lifeguard wanted to marry Silly Gilly, what would he be?
Her bathing suit-or.

Why didn't Silly Gilly understand the joke about the Grand Canyon?
It was too deep.

Why didn't she like the ocean joke?
She couldn't fathom it.

Why did Silly Gilly's boyfriend keep a stiff upper lip?

Someone starched his moustache.

Did Silly Gilly believe the story about the sleeping soldier?

No, it was a lot of bunk.

Did she believe the story about the sword?

No, she couldn't swallow it.

Why didn't Silly Gilly finish the book about the palace kidnapping?

Too many pages were missing.

Did Silly Gilly like the story about the bath towel?

Yes, it was absorbing.

How about the story about the snake trainers?

It was rather charming.

Did she like the story about the dog who chased the stick for two miles?

No, it was too far-fetched.

What did she say about the Venus de Milo story?

It was disarming.

Did Silly Gilly like the story about the drill?

She thought it was a bore!

Was she surprised at the story about the carpet?

Yes, it nearly floored her!

Did she believe the story about the sandwich?

No, it was full of baloney.

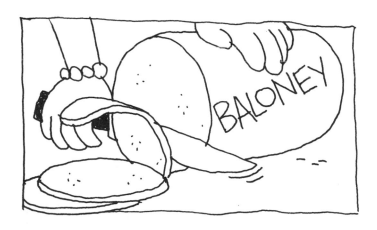

13 THE CART BEFORE THE HORSE

A: *Horse and buggy.*
Q: How do you feel when you have a sore throat and fleas?

A: *Polka.*
Q: What should you do when your sister falls asleep in church?

A: *General Hospital.*
Q: What has three stars, a lot of patients, and must be saluted every day?

A: *Fish cakes.*

Q: What do you give a shark for its birth-day?

A: *The whale spout.*

Q: How do you know when whales are sulking?

A: *"Piggyback!"*

Q: What did Kermit say when his girl-friend came home?

A: *A pigtail.*

Q: What is Miss Piggy's life story?

A: *Ignoramus.*
Q: What shall we do if Amos acts silly?

A: *Grammar school.*
Q: Is your grandmother hip?

A: *Tulane University.*
Q: What college teaches you how to drive on a divided highway?

A: *Molasses.*
Q: What do you get when you cross moles and donkeys?

A: *Banana splits.*
Q: What happens when a banana hears a good joke?

A: *Pandemonium.*

Q: What does a panda do when it hears a terrible joke?

A: *Needlepoint.*

Q: What goes on inside a compass?

A: *Milk pitcher, soup dish, and sugar bowl.*

Q: Name two containers and a football stadium.

A: *Chopsticks.*

Q: What happens to the lamb chop if you don't grease the pan?

A: *Egyptian mummy.*

Q: Who is married to an Egyptian daddy?

A: *Out of whack.*

Q: How does a tired baseball player feel?

STRIKE THREE!

A: *Neck and neck.*

Q: What would you see through the window of a giraffe's house?

A: *Football.*

Q: What do you call it if your toes have a good cry?

A: *Incognito.*

Q: What do you call a toe that's in disguise?

A: *Bermuda shorts.*

Q: What do they call elves in Bermuda?

A: *Himalayan.*

Q: What's the lazy boy doing in the hammock?

A: *An orangu-tan.*

Q: What does an ape get at the beach?

A: *Frostbite.*

Q: What must you beware of if you give a snowman false teeth?

A: *Snow belt.*

Q: What holds up a snowman's pants?

A: *Commentator.*
Q: What do you call a plain old potato?

A: *Paramount Pictures.*
Q: What do you call photos of Mt. Everest?

A: *Semi-sweet.*
Q: Is Sammy a good little baby?

A: *Hurdy-gurdy.*
Q: What did the hammer do when Gert hit her thumb with it?

A: *The apple core.*
Q: If a worm can't get into the Marine Corps, what can he join?

YOU NAME IT

What was the name of William Penn's brother?
Bic.

Who was Peeping Tom's sister?
Little Bo Peeping.

What did the rancher name his son?
Brandon.

If Millicent changes her name to Millie, what will happen?
She won't have a cent to her name.

What did Little Mary Sunshine name her baby?
Ray.

What did Snow White name her baby?
Egg.

What did Mrs. T. name her baby?
E.

What was the name of the car salesman?
Otto.

What was the name of Cinderella's fairy godmother?
Wanda.

PEOPLE, PLACES, & THINGS

Is the weather good in Brazil?
Yes, it's never Chile.

What happened when it rained on Uranus?
The Mercury fell, and Pluto Saturn a puddle.

Why is a flooded river like a large dictionary?
It's un-abridged.

What sizes do crowns come in?
King-size and queen-size.

What three-syllable word is always
mispronounced?
"Mispronounced."

Why is H the most popular letter?
It's the start of every holiday!

And why is O the cheeriest letter?
*It's always in a good mood and never
out of sorts.*

When is a lightbulb like a curious kid?
When it's 100 whats.

What goes over your head and under your feet but doesn't cover your body?

A jump rope.

When is a foot not a foot?

When it's ahead in a race.

What does a snowman put on his bed?

A sheet of ice and a blanket of snow.

Why do people say you saw wood when you snore?

Maybe because there's lumber in slumber.

Why is it dangerous to yawn at the beach?

You might get tongue tide.

DOUBLE TROUBLE

What do you need most when
you're waiting to see a doctor?
Patient's patience.

What would you like to wipe off
your eyeglasses?
Specs specks.

How did the scarecrow describe its
job?
Guardin' the garden.

What kind of canary does a
bargain hunter look for?
A cheaper cheeper.

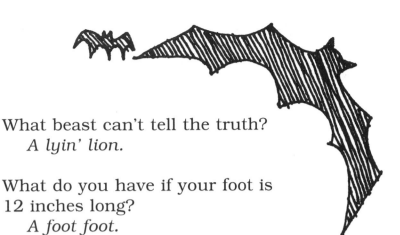

What beast can't tell the truth?
  A lyin' lion.

What do you have if your foot is
12 inches long?
  A foot foot.

What did the father of ten girls say
when another baby girl arrived?
  Alas—a lass!

What does Count Dracula have at the bank?
  A Count account.

What kind of lettuce do snowmen eat?
Iceberg.

What is the best thing to do before you take a bath?
Undress.

Where did the Old Lady Who Lived in a Shoe send her kids in the summer?
To boot camp.

What can you pay your teacher, even if you haven't a cent?
Attention.

What color is popular at football games?
Yell-ow.

Why is it so noisy in the forest?
The dogwood barks and the willow is weeping.

PURE CORN

In what bed is it perfectly okay to
dump manure?
A flower bed.

Why did the petunias want to move?
*They grew up in a seedy
neighborhood.*

What goes in one ear and out the
other?
A bug in a cornfield.

What do you get if a little bear
sits in the cornfield?
Corn on the cub.

What happens to cigars after dinner?
They meet their match.

Why are A and E the craziest vowels?
They're both in sane.

Why did the piggy bank yell "Ouch!"?
Because the miser pinched his pennies.

Why is T a generous letter?
Without it every mister would be a miser.

What's the difference between a new suit and a fireplace grate?
The suit looks great but the grate looks sooty.

What did the broom say to the vacuum cleaner?
"Don't you wish people would stop pushing us around?"

What happens when you don't dust your mirror?
It gives you a dirty look.

Here are some real toughies to try on the sharpest riddlers you know:

What do you find at supper in a Paris monastery?
An order of French friars.

What did the tailor get when he crossed a fireplace with a vegetable?
A three-peas soot.

What musical instrument does a frog play?
The hopsichord.

What do you get if you cross the Tower of Pisa with Miss Piggy?
Lean pork chops.

What do you get if you cross berries with a composer?
Raspberry Schubert.

What composer keeps the neighbors awake with his woof-ing?
Johann Sebastian Bark.

Why is it so noisy in a library during Christmas?
Because Lewis Carrolls.

How is a pushy person like your porch in winter?
They both get icy stares.

What bird was first to fly over the North Pole?
Admiral Richard Byrd.

What dessert took a stand at Little Big Horn?
General Custard.

Why did the little ghost's lemon meringue pie fly back and hit her?
It was a boo-meringue pie.

What's 5,600 feet tall and has four heads?
Mt. Rushmore.

What would you say if you were to meet the Dog Star in person?
"You can't be Sirius!"

What do you get if you cross a doorbell with a doughnut?
Ring around the cruller.

How is a large apartment like a candy store?
One is a suite of rooms; the other is a room of sweets.

What did the waitress say to the chef?
"Give me a little quiche!"

What's the difference between a man with a missing slipper and a detective trailing a criminal?

One suspects his dog and the other dogs his suspect.

Where do Russian ghosts live?
In Outer Mon-ghoulia.

What do you say to a skeleton crew when it goes sailing?
"Bone voyage!"

INDEX